2022

JUL

She
Persisted

MALALA YOUSAFZAI

—INSPIRED BY—

She Persisted

by Chelsea Clinton & Alexandra Boiger

. . . .

MALALA YOUSAFZAI

. . . .

Written by

Aisha Saeed

Interior illustrations by

Gillian Flint

PHILOMEL

PHILOMEL BOOKS
An imprint of Penguin Random House LLC, New York

First published in the United States of America by Philomel Books,
an imprint of Penguin Random House LLC, 2022

Visit us online at penguinrandomhouse.com.

Library of Congress Cataloging-in-Publication Data is available.

Printed in the United States of America

HC ISBN 9780593402917
10 9 8 7 6 5 4 3 2 1
PB ISBN 9780593402931
10 9 8 7 6 5 4 3 2 1

WOR

Edited by Jill Santopolo and Talia Benamy.
Design by Ellice M. Lee.
Text set in LTC Kennerley.

❧ To ❧
every kid who speaks up and
stands up for what is right

She
Persisted

....

She Persisted: WANGARI MAATHAI

She Persisted: WILMA MANKILLER

She Persisted: PATSY MINK

She Persisted: SALLY RIDE

She Persisted: MARGARET CHASE SMITH

She Persisted: SONIA SOTOMAYOR

She Persisted: MARIA TALLCHIEF

She Persisted: DIANA TAURASI

She Persisted: HARRIET TUBMAN

She Persisted: OPRAH WINFREY

She Persisted: MALALA YOUSAFZAI

DEAR READER,

As Sally Ride and Marian Wright Edelman both powerfully
said, "You can't be what you can't see." When Sally said that,
she meant that it was hard to dream of being an astronaut,
like she was, or a doctor or an athlete or anything at all if you
didn't see someone like you who already had lived that dream.
She especially was talking about seeing women in jobs that
historically were held by men.

I wrote the first *She Persisted* and the books that came
after it because I wanted young girls—and children of all
genders—to see women who worked hard to live their dreams.
And I wanted all of us to see examples of persistence in the face
of different challenges to help inspire us in our own lives.

I'm so thrilled now to partner with a sisterhood of
writers to bring longer, more in-depth versions of these stories
of women's persistence and achievement to readers. I hope
you enjoy these chapter books as much as I do and find them
inspiring and empowering.

And remember: If anyone ever tells you no, if anyone
ever says your voice isn't important or your dreams are too big,
remember these women. They persisted and so should you.

Warmly,
Chelsea Clinton

MALALA YOUSAFZAI

TABLE OF CONTENTS

....

Curious from the Start

On July 12, 1997, in the Pakistani city of Mingora, snug in the lush Swat Valley, a baby girl was born. Her father gazed down starry-eyed at his firstborn child and thought about the legendary Afghan poet Malalai of Maiwand, who was famous for her courage and convictions. He smiled and said he would name his daughter Malala.

Pakistan's Swat Valley is famous for its snow-

capped mountains, flower-filled meadows, and clear blue lakes. People travel from all over the world to vacation there. They hike the mountains, enjoy the local hospitality, and take part in the joyful summer festivals. Malala's early years were peaceful and happy in this scenic wonderland. She played with her friends and she also spent time with her two younger brothers (sometimes she arm wrestled them!). But even as a small child, Malala's favorite place to be was school. She felt at home there. Her father was a teacher and ran several schools for girls in their community. When she was very little, before she could even speak, she would wander into his classrooms while he was teaching. Sometimes she would even pretend to be the teacher!

As Malala continued to grow, both her

curiosity and love for learning grew as well. She spoke three different languages: Pashto, Urdu, and English. She was a hardworking student and loved going to school, learning new things, and being with her friends. She even loved the pens and notebooks with which she wrote down what she was learning. She often daydreamed about all the things she wanted to do when she grew up. She knew she wanted to help people, so she thought about becoming a doctor, and later, she thought she might want to become a politician. Malala greatly admired Benazir Bhutto, who had been Pakistan's first female prime minister—the leader of Pakistan's government. She thought that becoming a prime minster would be a job that could help her assist even more people than being a doctor would. Her father encouraged Malala to soar as high as her dreams could take her. Malala was grateful to her father for not "clipping her wings."

Malala loved school and was sad when she learned that not all children were as lucky as she was to attend classes and learn. One day, when Malala was young, she went to drop off garbage at the local dump. She winced at the strong smell and tried her best not to get her clothing and shoes dirty. As she neared the garbage, she saw that there were children digging through the trash. Malala was surprised and confused. A little girl sorted some of the rubbish and placed it in piles. A few boys were fishing for metal scraps among the heap.

The kids looked like they were Malala's age. She looked at the little girl, trying to remember her from any of her classes, but it didn't seem like the

girl went to her school. *Why haven't I seen her in my classes?* Malala wondered.

When she spoke to her father about the children she'd seen digging through the garbage, he explained to her that sadly not all children were able to attend school. The kids she saw digging through the trash were looking for things they might be able to sell for money. They would use the money to feed their families. Her father told her that this was the sad reality for millions of kids around the world, who have families so poor they need everyone in the household—even young kids—to work in order to survive.

Malala was very upset to learn about this. It was unfair that some kids were denied an opportunity to attend school and become whoever they wanted to be because of their life circumstances. All children, thought Malala, had the right to attend school.

On that day, as Malala thought about those children, she did not know that in just a short while, she herself would also be denied access to an education, the thing she cherished so very much. In fact, Malala could never have imagined just how dramatically everything in her life would soon change.

CHAPTER 2
....

Speaking Up

When Malala was ten years old, a group called the Taliban arrived in Mingora. They carried weapons with them and quickly took control over her town. The Taliban believed that girls and women did not have the right to do the same things as boys and men. With their arrival, Malala's entire world turned upside down. The Taliban banned anyone from own-ing a television, playing music, or dancing. They forbade women from shopping at stores.

Eventually, and most devastating of all for Malala, the Taliban also said that girls could not attend school. They shut down all the schools for girls in Malala's community, and eventually began to destroy schools by blowing them up.

The Taliban said that anyone who spoke out against them or didn't follow their orders would be hurt or killed. Anyone who disagreed with the Taliban lived in fear, worrying that they could be in danger.

The Taliban were Muslim and said they did this because of their religion, Islam. But Malala was also Muslim, and she knew what they were doing was not acceptable in her religion. She loved her faith, and found strength and peace from it. She also knew the true practice of Islam valued education and the rights of women. As difficult as it was to lose her access to an education, it was also hurtful to see these people claim to do the hateful things they did in the name of her beloved faith.

At eleven years old, Malala's eyes filled with tears as she said goodbye to her classmates and left her school. She wondered if she would ever have the chance to be in a classroom again. She looked on with frustration and sadness as the Taliban destroyed school after school in her area. In total, they destroyed about four hundred schools. The situation in her community eventually became so dangerous that Malala's family worried for their safety and had to flee their city for a while.

Slowly, as the Pakistani government began to push the Taliban out of the area, things grew a little safer, and Malala returned with her family back to her community. Schools also began to reopen, and Malala and other girls began to attend classes once more. Malala was grateful to attend school again, but even though the Taliban were not as powerful as they once were, they remained a threat. Many girls were still afraid to go to school. Someone had to do something, she thought. *Someone* had to say something and stand up to them. Maybe, Malala thought, that someone needed to be her. Malala hoped that if others in Pakistan and around the world knew what was happening and what the Taliban were doing, they would see how wrong it was and try to help. She decided it was time to use her voice and her words to bring attention to her situation.

On September 1, 2008, Malala gave a speech

in the nearby city of Peshawar about the injustice
taking place in her community. The title of her
speech was "How Dare the Taliban Take Away
My Basic Right to Education?" In her speech she
shared what was happening in Mingora and the

grave dangers her people were facing. Her speech was played on television sets around the country, and many people listened to Malala's message. They were moved that a child so young was so brave. She knew she risked angering the Taliban by speaking up about the injustices, but it did not stop her from saying the truth. And later that year, when the Taliban began shutting down schools and once again bombing them, her frustration grew more and more.

Shortly after her speech, a journalist from an international newspaper approached her father. The journalist asked if there was a student in his class who might be willing to anonymously— which means without using their real name, so they wouldn't be in danger—write about life under Taliban rule to help the world understand what was happening. It was hard to find someone willing to speak up. One girl volunteered, but her father thought it was too dangerous. People were scared that if they shared the truth about what the Taliban were doing, it would anger them. They knew they would be punished if the Taliban found out who was speaking up.

Malala knew it was important to share what was happening. Words have the power to bring truth to light, and Malala hoped that by speaking up about the difficulties she and her people faced, things could change. Malala began writing about what it was like to live under Taliban control. To protect her identity, she used the pseudonym—a made-up name—Gul Makai (which in the Pashto language means cornflower).

Writing as Gul Makai, Malala wrote about

the risks she took in order to attend school. She wrote about missing her friends who had to move away due to the threat the Taliban posed. Malala also wrote about how much she loved learning. When the Taliban found out about the anony-mous column, they were furious. They demanded to know the identity of the secret writer. Malala was scared, but she kept on writing. She knew they would punish her if they found out who Gul Makai really was, but she wasn't going to let them stop her from telling the truth.

In addition to her secret work, Malala began speaking publicly on television. She was featured in a film that explored her work as an activist for social change. Malala even met with the United States special envoy to Afghanistan—an American diplomat chosen to work on specific issues with the

Afghan government—about the problems regarding educating girls and the importance of education for everyone.

Praise for Malala's outspoken activism grew and grew. Desmond Tutu—a bishop and human rights activist—nominated her in October 2011 for the International Children's Peace Prize, and later that year she won Pakistan's first National Youth Peace Prize (now called the National Malala Peace Prize). The world was taking notice of Malala. And unfortunately, the Taliban were, too. They quickly realized that Malala was the girl secretly writing about their actions. They also realized Malala was not going to stop speaking up. So they decided to do something about it.

....

A Perilous Moment

October 9, 2012, was like most of the days before it. By then, Malala was fifteen years old. The Pakistani government had pushed back the Taliban control in her city, but there were still some who remained. Despite the lingering threat of the Taliban, Malala was grateful to be in school and learning with her friends once again.

That afternoon, Malala boarded her school bus after classes were over to head home. The

bus was a white Toyota truck with benches built into the sides and a canopy cover. She preferred to walk to and from school, but her mother thought traveling by bus would be safer. As the bus engine roared to life that day, Malala's mind was filled with thoughts about her exams. They were in the middle of a week of testing, and she was thinking about all the things she'd need to study to make sure she got good grades.

As the bus drove onward, Malala laughed and chatted with her friends Kainat, Shazia, and Moniba, who were also on the bus with her. Drawing closer to Malala's home, a funny feeling passed over the girls. Even though nothing was out of place, something felt strange. They noticed that the road was completely empty. There were no cars. There were no people.

Just then, two men appeared. One of her friends thought the men might be journalists who wanted to interview Malala about her brave work to print in a magazine or a newspaper. But the girls quickly realized that these two men were not journalists. Jumping onto the bus, the men angrily shouted: "Where is Malala?"

The girls were stunned. They glanced worriedly at Malala. Though they did not tell the men where Malala was, when the girls looked at her, they accidentally revealed who she was. Before anyone could do anything to protect her, one of the men shot Malala. He also attacked her friends Shazia and Kainat, who were both injured but survived.

Fighting for her life, Malala was quickly airlifted to a nearby hospital in Pakistan for emergency treatment. Her injury was very serious, and eventually she was taken by a special air ambulance to England for multiple surgeries that lasted many hours. The doctors had no idea if Malala would survive or if she would have long-lasting injuries, but they worked as hard as they could to save her life. News of what happened to Malala spread quickly around the world. Soon millions of people were watching and hoping and praying that Malala would be okay.

Malala had been unconscious after she was attacked. When she finally woke up seven days later, she could not speak because she had tubes in her mouth. She had no memory of what had happened to her, and she had no idea where she was.

She was shocked to learn that she had been shot by the Taliban. She knew they were angry about her activism, but she had no idea they would attack a child. She also was stunned to discover that she was no longer in her hometown of Mingora, Pakistan. She was at the Queen Elizabeth Hospital in Birmingham, England.

From her hospital bed, Malala watched the media coverage about her. She was astonished to learn that television stations, newspapers, and magazines from around the world were talking about what she had been through. She was touched by all the well wishes and prayers for her speedy recovery. Malala realized that her work and her bravery was an inspiration to people around the world.

························

A Choice

After months of surgeries and rehabilitation to help her get better, Malala slowly began to recover from her attack. The doctors all agreed she was very lucky to have survived and to have no major lasting damage.

Malala longed to return to her home in Mingora, her school, and her friends. But the Taliban warned that if she returned, they would try to kill her again. Though Malala was upset about this, she was also grateful for the opportunity for her new life with her parents and brothers in the United Kingdom.

Malala enrolled in school in England, and though she was happy to attend classes and learn

once again, everything was different from what she was used to back in Pakistan. Unlike the cozy school she'd known all her life, her new school building was huge and confusing, with many differently colored stairs leading in different directions. Her classwork felt more complicated, and she even got some bad grades. And unlike in Pakistan, where Malala had her friends whom she'd known her whole life, here she felt like an outsider. The other kids in her classes dressed and spoke differently from her. Malala sometimes felt lonely, but she persisted. She kept working hard and tried her best.

As she adjusted to her new life, Malala realized that she had an important decision to make. She could go to school and get an education and live her life quietly behind closed doors, or she could get her education and *also* do whatever she could with the life she'd been given to continue to speak up for kids around the world and their right to an education. Malala knew that even though she was now safer than she had been, millions of children around the world were not. There were many kids doing everything they could to get educated, and she decided she wanted to do what she could to speak up on their behalf and help them.

On July 12th, her sixteenth birthday, Malala went to the United Nations and gave a speech that was heard around the world. In her remarks, she said she would continue to speak up for the right of every child to receive an education. She told the audience that even though she was the one speaking at the United Nations, she was one of many other people like her who were fighting against

injustice. Malala said everyone had the right to live in peace, to be treated with dignity, to have equal opportunities, like the right to an education. She concluded her powerful speech by saying: *One child, one teacher, one pen, and one book can change the world. Education is the only solution. Education first.*

Malala's speech was so moving that everyone in the audience gave her a standing ovation—they stood up and applauded her words, her conviction, and her bravery. The United Nations declared July 12 "Malala Day," and it is celebrated each year in honor of her courage and her advocacy for education for all.

That same year, Malala also established a nonprofit charity called the Malala Fund with her father. The Malala Fund was created to push for the right for every girl to have twelve years of free, safe, quality education. It focuses on parts of the world where the most girls miss out on education after elementary school, including: Afghanistan, Brazil, Ethiopia, Lebanon, Nigeria, Pakistan, and Turkey. Malala's organization works with local educators and advocates from each area who know best the needs of their communities. The Malala Fund also works with governments at the local, national, and international levels to help girls get the education they deserve. The Malala Fund has also helped build schools around the world.

The Taliban tried to silence Malala. Instead her voice grew stronger.

·····························

Recognition

Malala was still a teenager, continuing with both schooling and her advocacy work, when on October 10, 2014, just over two years after her attack by the Taliban on her way home from school, she experienced another event that changed her life dramatically.

She was seventeen years old and still in high school in Birmingham, England. That morning, Malala was in the middle of a chemistry lesson

when one of her teachers walked into the class to
share an important message: Malala had just been
awarded the Nobel Peace Prize for her struggles
and advocacy for young people and their right to

education. Malala shared this award with Kailash Satyarthi, an activist from India who was also working tirelessly for education access for all children. Education is a way for millions of children to find a path out of poverty and difficult situations and to have a better and more peaceful life.

The Nobel Peace Prize is the most important award given to someone who has worked to encourage and promote peace among countries or groups of people anywhere in the world. The average age of the winner of this prize is sixty-two years old. Malala was not only the first Pakistani to ever receive the Nobel Peace Prize, but at seventeen years old, she was also the youngest person to ever receive it.

Malala was surprised and deeply moved by the unexpected honor. At first she was nervous to win such a huge award at such a young age, but she quickly realized that winning the Nobel Peace Prize was about more than just getting a medal to put up in her home. It was a message to Malala that she needed to keep up her advocacy and never stop believing in herself and her work. After winning the Nobel Peace Prize, Malala hoped she could continue to get support from people and organizations around the world to fulfill her dream of a future where every child was able to get a quality education.

In fact, Malala believed in education so much that even though she'd won the Nobel Peace Prize that day, she did not leave school early to celebrate. Instead Malala continued on to her physics and English classes and finished her school day!

When Malala officially accepted her award, in

Oslo, Norway, on December 10, 2014, she thanked her teachers and her parents, and she expressed gratitude to her faith of Islam for teaching her to be patient and to always speak the truth. She joked about how she was probably the only Nobel Peace Prize recipient who still fought with her little brothers. Malala told the audience that she shared her story with the world not because what she had been through was unique but because it was not. Malala's story was the story of so many others who might never see their names in headlines but who were fighting in the name of justice and peace regardless of the personal risks they faced in doing so. Malala urged those listening to her speech to not feel sorry for kids who were struggling, but to use how they felt to inspire themselves to do something to help those kids. She wanted all people to be the change they wanted to see in the world. Malala hoped to one day live in a world where no child would be deprived of an education, and she hoped that, by winning this award, she would gain more support and the ability to see her dream come true.

··· 38 ···

....

The Work Continues

After winning the Noble Prize, Malala continued attending high school. Alongside studying for exams and doing her homework, she kept working with the Malala Fund to shine a light on the important human rights issue of education for girls. She also published books about her own story and the stories of others who have had to leave their homes and haven't been able to return safely.

After graduating from high school, Malala decided to go to college. She studied philosophy, politics, and economics at the University of Oxford in England. Oxford University is the same college that Benazir Bhutto, the first female prime minster of Pakistan, attended. Malala had admired her as a

child, and now as an adult she was able to attend the very same school as her hero.

Malala loved college. She enjoyed making new friends and learning more about the world around her. She felt that attending college helped her to develop the ability to think deeply about important matters and to see things in new ways.

Malala graduated from Oxford in 2020 during the global COVID-19 pandemic. A pandemic happens when there's an illness that spreads throughout a whole country or the world. COVID-19 had spread throughout the entire globe and, in order to avoid getting sick, many people stopped traveling, attending school in person, or doing many things they normally did. Malala's plans were also affected by the pandemic and so, like many others, she paused to figure out what her next

steps would be once the pandemic ended. She was not exactly sure what she would do, but she did know that there were still approximately 130 million girls out of school around the world. She knew that her work was not yet done. And that it was just as important as it ever had been to fight for a more equal and just world for all.

Malala is now a household name, and kids in classrooms all over the world know her story. Though there were so many challenges and obstacles in her path, Malala knew what was important and what she believed in, and she did everything she could to work toward her dreams to create a better world. Malala persisted, and no matter what is important to you, never forget that persistence is the key to seeing dreams come true.

HOW YOU CAN PERSIST

by Aisha Saeed

Malala values education and the importance of doing whatever we can to make the world a better place. Here are some ways you can make a difference in your community and persist like Malala:

1. Have a bake sale and raise money to support the Malala Fund.

2. Tutor a young neighbor or a sibling on a subject they need help in.

3. Put together a Little Free Library in your community, or donate your old books to an existing one to support and pass on the love of reading and books.

4. Share Malala's story with someone and talk about what you can do to make the world a better place.

5. Make a list of all the things *you* feel would help to make the world a better place. Pick one thing from the list and look up ways that you can do something about it.

6. Start a book club about Malala and discuss her life and achievements.

ACKNOWLEDGMENTS

Thank you, Jill Santopolo and Talia Benamy, for your help and insight with this story. Thank you, Alexandra Boiger and Gillian Flint, for the beautiful illustrations. Thank you as well to the entire team at Penguin Random House. Thank you, Chelsea Clinton, for creating this series and reminding us of the many brave and fearless women who inspire all of us. Malala's bravery and persistence have been a personal inspiration for me and my work—my middle grade novel *Amal Unbound* was inspired in part by the bravery and persistence of Malala—so I am very honored and grateful I was able to share Malala's story with you.

❧ *References* ❧

Allen, Jonathon. "Malala Yousafzai Speaks of
Nobel Hopes." *Reuters.* October 11, 2013.
reuters.com/article/us-usa-nobel-malala
/malala-yousafzai-speaks-of-nobel-hopes
-idUSBRE99A03Q20131011.

Blumberg, Naomi. "Malala Yousafzai."
Encyclopedia Britannica. July 8, 2021.
britannica.com/biography/Malala-Yousafzai.

Felton, Lena. "Malala Yousafzai Just Graduated.
Now She Wants You to Join Her Feminist
Book Club." *The Lily*. August 19, 2020. thelily
.com/malala-yousafzai-just-graduated-now-she
-wants-you-to-join-her-feminist-book-club.

Guggenheim, Davis. *He Named Me Malala*.
Abu Dhabi: Imagenation Abu Dhabi FZ. 2015.
Film, 1:28:00.

Kettler, Sara. "Malala Yousafzai Biography."
Biography.com. April 2, 2014. biography.com
/activist/malala-yousafzai.

"Malala's Story." Malala Fund. Accessed
September 18, 2021. malala.org/malalas-story.

"Malala Yousafzai." The Nobel Prize. Accessed
September 18, 2021. nobelprize.org/prizes
/peace/2014/yousafzai/lecture.

"Malala Yousafzai Learns of Nobel Win while
Sitting in Chemistry Class." *The Guardian.*
October 10, 2014. theguardian.com/world
/2014/oct/10/malala-yousafzai-learns-of
-nobel-win-while-sitting-in-chemistry-class.

"Moving Moments from Malala's BBC Diary."
BBC. October 10, 2014. bbc.com/news
/world-asia-29565738.

"Nomination and Selection of Nobel Peace
Prize Laureates." The Nobel Prize. Accessed

September 19, 2021. nobelprize.org/nomination
/peace. "Taliban." *Britannica Kids.* Accessed
September 19, 2021. kids.britannica.com/kids
/article/Taliban/627261#.

Walsh, Declan. "Taliban Gun Down Girl Who
Spoke Up for Rights." *New York Times.*
October 9, 2012. nytimes.com/2012/10/10
/world/asia/teen-school-activist-malala
-yousafzai-survives-hit-by-pakistani-taliban.html.

Yousafzai, Malala, and Patricia McCormick.
*I Am Malala: How One Girl Stood Up for
Education and Changed the World (Young
Readers Edition).* New York: Little, Brown
Books for Young Readers, 2016.

Yousafzai, Malala. *Malala's Magic Pencil*. New York: Little, Brown Books for Young Readers, 2017.

Yousafzai, Malala. *We are Displaced: My Journey and Stories from Refugee Girls Around the World*. New York: Little, Brown Books for Young Readers, 2019.

Yousafzai, Malala. "Malala Yousafzai: Our Books and Our Pens Are the Most Powerful Weapons." United Nations Youth Assembly. New York, New York. July 12, 2013. Transcript. theguardian.com/commentisfree/2013/jul/12/malala-yousafzai-united-nations-education-speech-text.

Yousafzai, Malala. "Malala Yousafzai BBC
Interview." Interview by Mishal Husain. BBC.
October 7, 2013. Video, 9:30. bbc.com/news
/av/world-asia-24435564.

Yousafzai, Malala. "Malala Yousafzai Nobel
Lecture." Filmed December 10, 2014, at
Oslo City Hall, Oslo, Norway. Video 28:42.
nobelprize.org/prizes/peace/2014/yousafzai
/lecture.

Yousafzai, Malala. "We Are Supported by . . .
Malala Yousafzai." Interview by Kristen Bell
and Monica Padman. *We Are Supported
By*. Armchair Expert. June 30, 2021. Audio,
1:15:05. armchairexpertpod.com/pods
/malala-yousafzai.

AISHA SAEED is an award-winning and *New York Times* bestselling author of books for children. Her middle grade novel *Amal Unbound* (Penguin) received multiple starred reviews and was a Global Read Aloud for 2018. Her picture book, *Bilal Cooks Daal* (Simon and Schuster), received an APALA honor. Aisha is also a founding member of the nonprofit We Need Diverse Books™. She lives in Atlanta, Georgia, with her family.

You can visit Aisha online at
aishasaeed.com
and follow her on Twitter and Instagram
@aishacs

GILLIAN FLINT has worked as a professional illustrator since earning an animation and illustration degree in 2003. Her work has since been published in the UK, USA and Australia. In her spare time, Gillian enjoys reading, spending time with her family and puttering about in the garden on sunny days. She lives in the northwest of England.

You can visit Gillian Flint online at
gillianflint.com
or follow her on Twitter
@GillianFlint
and on Instagram
@gillianflint_illustration

CHELSEA CLINTON is the author of the #1 *New York Times* bestseller *She Persisted: 13 American Women Who Changed the World*; *She Persisted Around the World: 13 Women Who Changed History*; *She Persisted in Sports: American Olympians Who Changed the Game*; *Don't Let Them Disappear: 12 Endangered Species Across the Globe*; *It's Your World: Get Informed, Get Inspired & Get Going!*; *Start Now!: You Can Make a Difference*; with Hillary Clinton, *Grandma's Gardens* and *Gutsy Women*; and, with Devi Sridhar, *Governing Global Health: Who Runs the World and Why?* She is also the Vice Chair of the Clinton Foundation, where she works on many initiatives, including those that help empower the next generation of leaders. She lives in New York City with her husband, Marc, their children and their dog, Soren.

You can follow Chelsea Clinton on Twitter
@ChelseaClinton
or on Facebook at
facebook.com/chelseaclinton

ALEXANDRA BOIGER has illustrated nearly twenty picture books, including the She Persisted books by Chelsea Clinton; the popular Tallulah series by Marilyn Singer; and the Max and Marla books, which she also wrote. Originally from Munich, Germany, she now lives outside of San Francisco, California, with her husband, Andrea, daughter, Vanessa, and two cats, Luiso and Winter.

Photo credit: *Vanessa Blasich*

You can visit Alexandra Boiger online at
alexandraboiger.com
or follow her on Instagram
@alexandra_boiger

Read about more inspiring women in the

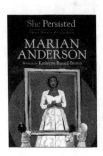

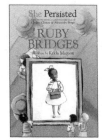

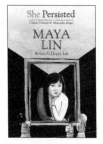

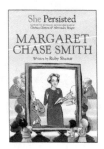

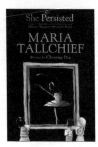

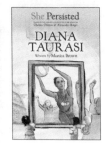

She Persisted series!

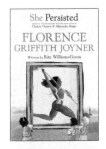

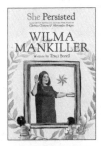

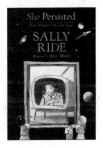

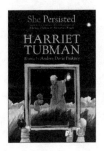
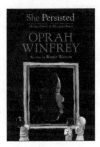
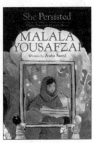